Northwest
Territories

Northwest Territories

Richard W. Daitch

Lerner Publications Company

LIBRARY OF CONGRESS
CATALOGING-IN-PUBLICATION DATA

Daitch, Richard W.
    Northwest Territories / by Richard W. Daitch.
        p. cm. — (Hello Canada)
    Includes index.
    ISBN 0–8225–2761–8 (lib. bdg.)
    1. Northwest Territories—Juvenile literature.
    I. Title. II. Series.
F1060.35.D35 1996
971.9′2—dc20   95–4222
                                                    CIP
                                                    AC

Cover photograph by Ned Therrien. Background photo by R. Chen/SuperStock.

Every effort has been made to contact the copyright holders of the material quoted in this book. Any omissions that are brought to our attention will be acknowledged and credited in subsequent printings of this book.

The glossary on page 68 gives definitions of words shown in **bold type** in the text.

Senior Editor
Gretchen Bratvold
Editors
Domenica Di Piazza
Colleen Sexton
Photo Researcher
Cindy Hartmon Nelson
Designer
Steve Foley

Our thanks to Jean-Marie Beaulieu, Social Studies Curriculum Coordinator for the Department of Education, Culture and Employment, Government of the Northwest Territories, for his help in preparing this book.

Manufactured in the United States of America
1 2 3 4 5 6 – JR – 01 00 99 98 97 96

 This book is printed on acid-free, recyclable paper.

Contents

Fun Facts

🍁 Imagine playing baseball on Ellesmere Island. If you started the game in June, it wouldn't have to be called off because of darkness until September! That's because the Northwest Territories lies so far north that the sun lights the sky for most of the summer.

🍁 The Northwest Territories has eight official languages—Inuktitut, French, English, Slavey, Dogrib, Chipewyan, Cree, and Gwich'in.

🍁 In 1992 residents of the Northwest Territories voted to divide the territory in two. The new eastern territory will be known as Nunavut.

Hi! My name is Barkley. As you read *Northwest Territories,* I will be helping you make sense of some of the maps and charts that appear in the book.

A glacier carved this deep swirl along a mountainside on Baffin Island.

🍁 More than 10,000 **glaciers** (masses of slowly moving ice) are found on Baffin Island in the eastern part of the Northwest Territories.

🍁 Great Bear Lake in the northwestern corner of the Northwest Territories is the largest lake lying entirely within Canada.

🍁 Ellesmere Island National Park is Canada's northernmost park.

🍁 Virginia Falls in the Northwest Territories' Nahanni National Park is nearly twice as high as Niagara Falls.

🍁 The Northwest Territories has the fastest growing population in Canada!

7

Canada's Last Frontier

Located in Canada's far north, the Northwest Territories is one of North America's last wilderness areas. With majestic mountains, winding rivers, deep valleys, rushing waterfalls, pine forests, and ice-capped Arctic islands, the Northwest Territories is a land of breathtaking beauty.

The borders of the Northwest Territories are as varied as the landscape. Mountains separate the Northwest Territories from its western neighbor, the Yukon Territory. The northern boundary of the Northwest Territories is only 500 miles (804 kilometers) from the icy North Pole. To the northeast, across Baffin Bay, is the country of Kalaallit Nunaat (Greenland). A huge inland sea called Hudson Bay lies to the southeast of the Northwest Territories.

Steep waterfalls (facing page), ***rugged mountains*** (above), ***and icy landscapes*** (right) ***are all part of the spectacular scenery in the Northwest Territories.***

Rocky land covers much of the Northwest Territories.

The Northwest Territories has seven southern neighbors. The northern coasts of Newfoundland and Québec meet the shores of a narrow body of water called the Hudson Strait. Across Hudson Bay lies the province of Ontario. The Northwest Territories' other southern neighbors are the provinces of Manitoba, Saskatchewan, Alberta, and British Columbia.

About three-fourths of the Northwest Territories is part of the Canadian Shield, a rocky region that stretches across much of Canada. Thousands of years ago, the Shield was covered by **ice caps**. These thick layers of ice scoured the land and gouged deep cracks and holes in the surface of the rock. When the **Ice Age** ended about 10,000 years ago, melting ice from glaciers filled the cracks. This water eventually formed lakes and **fjords** (deep, narrow sea inlets).

Nowadays the Northwest Territories has three main geographic regions—the Arctic Mainland, the Mackenzie Valley, and the Arctic Islands. The Arctic Mainland in the east

and the Mackenzie Valley in the west form the vast mainland of the Northwest Territories. To the north is the Arctic Islands region.

Most of the Northwest Territories lies above the tree line. North of this imaginary map line, the climate is too cold and dry for trees to grow. But the Mackenzie Valley is warmer, and pine and spruce trees provide supplies of timber. The region also holds minerals such as gold, natural gas, and oil. Nearly two-thirds of the Northwest Territories' inhabitants live in the Mackenzie Valley.

Giant spruce trees thrive in Wood Buffalo National Park. Three-fifths of Canada's national parklands are in the Northwest Territories.

The drawing of the Northwest Territories to the right is called a physical map. It shows physical features such as mountains, flatlands, rivers, and lakes. The colors represent a range of elevations, or heights above sea level (see legend box). This map also outlines each of the Northwest Territories' geographic regions. The map on this page, called a political map, mainly locates features created by people, including cities, roads, railways, and parks.

NORTHWEST TERRITORIES Political Map

| 0 | 150 | 300 | 450 | 600 km |
| 0 | 100 | 200 | 300 | 400 mi |

Ellesmere Island National Park

Resolute

Nanisivik

Inuvik

Cambridge Bay

Auyuittuq National Park

Norman Wells

Coppermine

Gjoa Haven

Pangnirtung

Nahanni National Park

Deline (Fort Franklin)

Hall Beach

Bathurst Inlet

Fort Simpson

Rae-Edzo

Baker Lake

Iqaluit

Fort Liard

⊛Yellowknife

Cape Dorset

HayRiver

Fort Resolution

Fort Smith

Rankin Inlet

Wood Buffalo National Park

Arviat

12

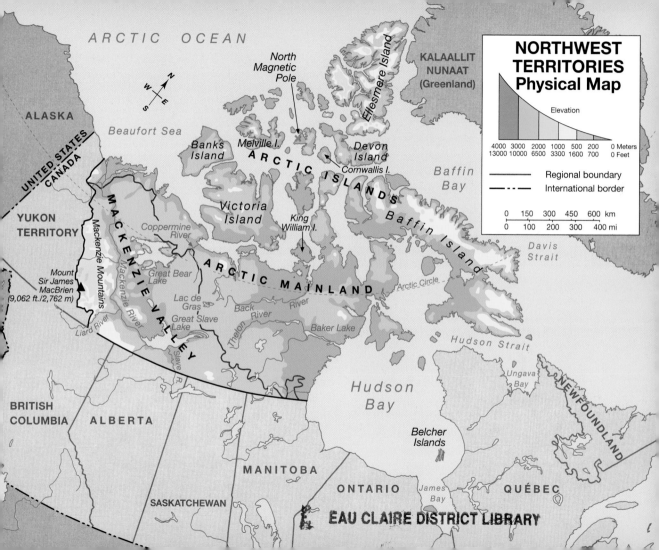

The wide Mackenzie River (facing page) *flows along the base of the Mackenzie Mountains* (above) *in the western Northwest Territories.*

The rugged Mackenzie Mountains rise along the far western edge of the Mackenzie Valley region. These peaks are part of the Rocky Mountain system, which stretches all the way into the southwestern United States. Mount Sir James MacBrien, the highest peak in the Mackenzie range, reaches 9,062 feet (2,762 meters).

Many rivers and lakes lie in the Mackenzie Valley. The Coppermine River flows north 525 miles (845 km) into the Arctic Mainland region. Even longer is the mighty Mackenzie River, Canada's lengthiest waterway. The Mackenzie snakes its way northwest from Great Slave Lake to the Beaufort Sea—an arm of the Arctic Ocean. Great Bear Lake, covered with ice for most of the year, is the eighth largest lake in the world.

Perched on the shore of Great Slave Lake, Yellowknife (left) *is the northernmost city in North America. In summer green grass covers the Arctic Mainland* (facing page right). *Patches of salmonberries* (facing page left) *add color to this tundra region, where the land is rocky and treeless.*

About half of the people in the Mackenzie Valley live in or near Yellowknife, the capital of the Northwest Territories. Other large communities include Inuvik, Hay River on the south shore of Great Slave Lake, and Fort Smith, which is located near the Alberta border.

The Arctic Mainland is a region of rocky, treeless **tundra.** Only a few types of plants, such as hardy grasses, mosses, and lichens grow here. The permanently frozen ground of the tundra is called **permafrost.** In the summer, a thin layer of the surface soil thaws. Then arctic poppies, purple saxifrage, dwarf fireweed, yellow cinquefoil, and other colorful wildflowers bloom.

Many lakes and long rivers, including the Back, the Coppermine, and the Thelon Rivers, are located on the Arctic Mainland. Although the region has minerals such as nickel, gold, uranium, oil, and gas, many of the resources remain untapped. Major communities in the Arctic Mainland include Baker Lake, Rankin Inlet, Coppermine, and Arviat. Many of the Inuit residents in this region rely on fishing, hunting caribou, and selling their artworks to make a living.

Learning about Permafrost

The students in John Jamieson's class at Thomas Simpson School in Fort Simpson wanted to learn more about permafrost. So they studied three locations—one close to the school, the second in an open field some distance away, and the third in a deeply forested area nearby. Placing soil probes into the ground, the students measured the temperature of the soil over several months. They found that the earth near the school was always above 32° F (0° C), the freezing point. The heat given off by the school building helped keep the soil warm and prevented permafrost from forming.

The students discovered a big difference between the open field and the forested area. During the summer, the field thawed completely while the forested area had 3 feet (1 meter) of permafrost year-round. The students concluded that permafrost occurs in cold regions that are also protected, like the forest, by trees or other objects that prevent the sun from warming the earth.

The Arctic Islands region is made up of numerous islands in the Arctic Ocean, north of the mainland. Iqaluit, on Baffin Island, is the largest community in the region. Farther north, on Ellesmere Island, lies Mount Barbeau—one of the highest peaks in the Northwest Territories. All of the islands in the Hudson, James, and Ungava Bays to the east of the mainland also belong to the Northwest Territories.

Temperatures on the northern islands are some of the coldest in the Northwest Territories. Winters are frigid throughout the territory, with average Arctic Mainland temperatures of about –25° F (–32° C). In general residents of the Mackenzie Valley enjoy warmer temperatures. In the summer, temperatures in the region hover around 69° F (21° C). But in the Arctic community

Explorers often start their journey to the North Pole from Resolute, a community on Cornwallis Island.

of Iqaluit, the average July temperature is only about 50° F (10° C).

Overall, the Northwest Territories is dry. The annual amount of **precipitation** (rain and melted snow) in the Mackenzie Valley ranges from 9 inches (23 centimeters) to 15 inches (38 cm). The northernmost parts of the Arctic Islands receive so little precipitation— less than 5 inches (13 cm)—that they are considered **deserts.**

Sightseers float past an iceberg. These huge chunks of ice break off glaciers and melt slowly as they drift southward.

The Northwest Territories is home to many kinds of wildlife. Whales swim in the chilly waters off the Arctic coast. Walrus lumber across the coastal Arctic ice. In winter, polar bears wait to catch seals at holes in the ice, where the sea mammals come up for air.

Caribou travel in herds across the territory. On the tundra, musk oxen feed on grasses and low-growing shrubs. Huge wood buffalo live in Wood Buffalo National Park—a large, forested area that straddles the border between the Northwest Territories and Alberta. Grizzly bears, black bears, moose, beavers, foxes, wolves, marten, hare, and muskrats also make their homes in the territory.

Walruses (left) *use their ivory tusks to dig shellfish from the bottom of the Arctic Ocean. Eagles* (facing page left) *soar across the skies of the southern Northwest Territories. Arctic foxes* (facing page right) *live in the territory's tundra regions.*

All sorts of birds flock to the Northwest Territories. Seabirds such as gulls, eiders, jaegers, terns, guillemots, and murres, nest along the coasts. Snow geese, swans, and sandhill cranes live in swampy areas and near rivers. Residents often spot white pelicans, loons, falcons, eagles, snowy owls, and even rare whooping cranes. During summer, the birds feast on the billions of black flies and mosquitoes that breed in the territory. But these pests aren't as popular with the people of the Northwest Territories!

Early Dene tracked game through thick forests (left) *in summer and across frozen lakes* (below) *in winter.*

Settling an Icy Land

Aboriginal groups lived in what is now the Northwest Territories for thousands of years before Europeans set foot in the area. About 8,000 years ago, ancestors of modern-day Dene occupied the vast southern mainland between what are now Alaska and Hudson Bay.

These peoples gathered wild plants and berries for food and medicine. Using bows and arrows, they hunted moose and bear. Fishers made nets, hooks and lines, and stone weirs (fences built across streams) to catch their prey.

Long before refrigerators were invented, the Dene had methods for preserving food. In the fall, they dried moose, buffalo, and caribou meat and pounded it with a mixture of berries and fat to make pemmican. This long-lasting food could be eaten all winter. Fish also were dried for later use.

During winter, travel on foot in the deep snow became impossible. The Dene used snowshoes, sleds, and toboggans pulled by dog teams to cross the land. When winter ended and the sun melted the ice on rivers and lakes, the Dene traveled by canoe.

The Dene lived in tepees constructed from the hides of caribou or moose. In some areas, people built log houses, partly covering them with earth or snow to keep out harsh winds. During summer, groups of Dene gathered to play games, sing, and tell stories. Because the Dene had no written language, storytelling was the way children were taught their history and traditions.

The first people to settle in the Arctic regions were the Pre-Dorset. Around 2000 B.C., these distant ancestors of the

Pre-Dorset people cut and stacked blocks of snow to make their dome-shaped winter homes. Lamps lit inside the shelters provided heat and light.

Inuit left what is now Alaska and traveled across the Arctic. Over time, some groups went as far east as Greenland.

The Pre-Dorset people hunted seals, caribou, musk oxen, and walrus. They ate the meat of the animals and carved weapons and tools from walrus tusks and caribou antlers. In winter the Pre-Dorsets lived in snowhouses made from blocks of firmly packed snow. When the weather warmed up, the people stayed in animal-skin tents.

The Dorset people, descendants of the Pre-Dorsets, used dogsleds to trek across the snow. They traveled on rivers and lakes in small, skin-covered boats called kayaks. The Dorsets relied on walrus, whales, and fish for food.

Most groups of Dorset people disappeared from the Arctic around A.D. 1000, when the Thule people moved from what is now Alaska to the Arctic Islands. The Thule were hunters. Traveling in kayaks and large, open boats called umiaks, they speared fish and harpooned whales. Craftspeople made tools from the bones, tusks, skins, and sinews (tendons) of animals.

Meanwhile, Norse explorers from Iceland and Greenland came to what is

In the summer, the Thule traveled and fished in large sturdy boats called umiaks.

now the Northwest Territories in search of new land. But the Europeans didn't stay. Hundreds of years passed before other explorers arrived in the region.

In 1576 British sea captain Martin Frobisher landed on Baffin Island. He was looking for the Northwest Passage, a westward water route from Europe to Asia. Although Frobisher didn't find the passage, he claimed Baffin Island for England in 1577.

Around 1600 some Thule groups moved inland to track caribou, and the Inuit culture began to develop. Over the years, eight main Inuit groups evolved. The Caribou Inuit lived inland near Baker Lake and relied on caribou for food, shelter, and tools. The other groups were coastal peoples, who fished and hunted seals, whales, and walrus.

Martin Frobisher's Folly

British explorer Martin Frobisher is remembered for his voyages of exploration in the 1500s. But he didn't go down in history as either the world's greatest geologist or most successful prospector.

While exploring Baffin Island in 1576, Frobisher found rocks with golden flecks. Certain that he had found gold, he took the samples back to England, where Queen Elizabeth I gave him money for two more voyages.

Thinking he would earn a fortune, Frobisher brought large amounts of the glittering rocks back to England. But when he returned, scientists discovered that the rocks were worthless. Frobisher had not discovered gold at all. He had returned to England with a ship filled only with iron pyrites, or fool's gold!

While some explorers headed for the Arctic looking for the Northwest Passage, other Europeans came for furs. In 1670 a fur-trading firm called the Hudson's Bay Company was formed in Great Britain. The king of Britain gave the company the right to trade in Rupert's Land—an area that included a huge region of land around Hudson Bay. British fur traders soon began setting up trading posts in Rupert's Land.

Working for the Hudson's Bay Company, British explorer Samuel Hearne traveled down the long Coppermine River to the Arctic Ocean in 1770. During the two-year journey, Hearne found few fur-bearing animals on the tundra.

In 1789 an explorer named Alexander Mackenzie set out from Fort Chipewyan in what is now northern Alberta. Working for a fur-trading business called the North West Company, he canoed north to Great Slave Lake. From there he traveled down the river that now bears his name until he reached the Beaufort Sea. Mackenzie found that the forests along the river were filled with foxes and other fur-bearing animals.

Gradually fur-trading posts were opened throughout the North. Life wasn't easy at these posts. The traders worked hard and learned to adjust to the harsh climate. Far from home, the men often were lonely. Many married Aboriginal women, had families, and stayed in the Northwest Territories. Their children and descendants are known as Métis. Like their parents, many Métis also relied on the fur trade to make a living.

Furs in hand, Inuit hunters greet European traders arriving on a Hudson's Bay Company ship. The Europeans exchanged metal tools and other goods for the pelts.

Using sharp spears called harpoons, crews killed whales from small boats and then towed the dead animals to nearby ships.

Around this time, people from the United States and Europe were making a fortune hunting whales in the eastern Arctic. Whale oil was in high demand for lighting streetlamps and for making soap, paint, and varnish. Long plates of baleen from the mouths of whales were used in fishing rods, corsets, and buggy whips.

The whalers hired Inuit as boat pilots, hunters, and dogsled drivers. Although Inuit earned money from these jobs, they also caught diseases from the whalers. Europeans unknowingly passed on illnesses such as measles, typhus, and scarlet fever, which killed many people throughout the region.

Meanwhile, Europeans continued to explore the Arctic in search of the Northwest Passage. One of the most famous explorers was John Franklin, a British captain who led three expeditions to the Arctic between 1819 and 1845. On the final voyage, Franklin's ships became trapped in the ice near King William Island. By 1848 Franklin and his crew had died from starvation, disease, or overexposure to the cold.

Many expeditions were sent to try to find the Franklin expedition. During these searches, rescue teams mapped much of the Arctic. In 1857 one team found a cairn (mound of stones). Inside was a note reporting that Franklin had died 10 years earlier.

In 1870 the Hudson's Bay Company sold Rupert's Land to the Dominion of Canada. Canada combined Rupert's Land with the North-western Territory, which lay to the north and west. Together the two joined the Dominion as the North-West Territories. By 1880 the Arctic Islands also had become part of the North-West Territories.

British explorer John Franklin (right) *mapped much of the Canadian Arctic in the 1800s.*

Finding the Northwest Passage

For hundreds of years, European explorers had searched for a waterway from the Atlantic Ocean to the Pacific Ocean through the icy waters of Canada's Arctic region. In 1903 Norwegian explorer Roald Amundsen and his crew set sail on their ship, the *Gjoa*. They sucessfully completed their journey in 1906, finally solving the mystery of the Northwest Passage.

ARCTIC OCEAN

GREENLAND

CANADA

PACIFIC OCEAN

ATLANTIC OCEAN

▪ ▪ ▪ Northwest Passage

Missionaries to Miners

In 1903 the Canadian government sent the Royal Canadian Mounted Police to the North-West Territories to help strengthen the Dominion's claim to the region. By 1905 two new provinces—Alberta and Saskatchewan—had been carved from parts of the territory. The borders of what is now the Northwest Territories were decided in 1912.

Over the years, the population of the Northwest Territories steadily increased. Fur traders, teachers, and **missionaries** moved to the area from other parts of Canada and from Europe. The missionaries came to teach the Christian religion to Aboriginal peoples. The missionaries also built the first schools and hospitals in the territory.

In the late 1800s, a missionary named Edmund Peck created an alphabet for the Inuktitut language so Inuit could write. Until this time, Inuktitut was a spoken language only.

33

Many Inuit and Dene children went to mission schools, where they practiced the Christian religion and learned how to read and write.

Dene and Inuit children who attended mission schools became the first formally educated Aboriginal people in the Northwest Territories. Many of these children were taken to schools far from home. They missed their families. The students had to get used to a new language and strict discipline. Many of the children gradually forgot their own traditions and cultural values.

Missionaries were not the only newcomers to the Northwest Territories. Miners headed north after oil was discovered at Norman Wells in the Mackenzie Valley in 1920. To gain control of these mineral-rich lands, the Canadian government signed **treaties** (agreements) with the Dene. In return for land, officials promised the Dene money, medicine, and **reserves**—or territory to be used only by the Dene.

JIM KILABUK REMEMBERS

In Pangnirtung in 1983, an Inuit elder named Jim Kilabuk looked back on his boyhood on Blacklead Island in Cumberland Sound. He spoke of the time before the arrival of Europeans, when life was lived as it had been for hundreds of years. He spoke of shamans, or people with special powers to do good or ill for the people.

"I was born on Blacklead Island near the blue water of Taluttarusirk Bay in 1901. My father sometimes told me stories. Stories were the way we learned about our past. We didn't have history books. I liked the stories about shamans and ghosts best. From Father I learned that there are good and evil shamans, just like there are good and evil ordinary people.

"Once, the snow fell for so many days that hunters were unable to leave camp. As the snow grew higher, the people became hungrier. Just in time, a shaman was called. He flew to the sky and plugged a hole in a cloud where an evil shaman had been shoveling snow.

"There was a shaman, at a camp near Baker Lake, who had great powers. He cured the sick like doctors do today. Once, he even brought a young boy back to life after he died.

"There were six shamans on Blacklead Island when I was a boy. I knew them all. My favorite shaman was Kitturiaq. He was a good shaman who used his powers to cure the ill and help the hunters find animals when they were scarce. He had a ghost for a wife. Of course, no one could see her, but we often heard Kitturiaq talk to her. Their children, too, were invisible.

"You had to tell a shaman the truth, because he knew right away if you were lying. Once, a man asked Kitturiaq to cure his sick child. 'Tell me if you have done anything bad,' said Kitturiaq. The man said he had done nothing wrong. The child grew much worse. Kitturiaq told the man, 'Tell me the truth or your child will die.' The man confessed that he had stolen something. Only then could Kitturiaq cure the child.

"This was all long ago on Blacklead Island, but I remember everything. People led happy lives. I remember the dogs, ghosts, my mother, my father, Kitturiaq. I remember the high mountain Umanakjuak and the blue water of Taluttarusirk Bay. I remember it all."

In the 1930s, more people arrived in the Northwest Territories to mine radium and uranium near Great Bear Lake. The quiet town of Yellowknife boomed after gold was discovered in Yellowknife Bay in 1933.

During World War II (1939–1945), the U.S. military convinced Canadians to build the Canol Pipeline. The pipeline carried oil from Norman Wells to a refinery in the Yukon Territory. Here the crude (raw) oil was purified

In 1933 miners (left) *began working at Port Radium, which became one of the world's largest suppliers of radium. During World War II, U.S. troops* (right) *helped set up an oil pipeline. The oil was processed into fuel for military airplanes.*

for making gasoline and other oil products. The United States needed the fuel for military aircraft and other wartime equipment. The pipeline created jobs, and workers from Canada and the United States soon settled in the Mackenzie Valley.

Other communities grew during the war, too. On Baffin Island, the town of Frobisher Bay (now called Iqaluit) got its start as a U.S. Air Force landing strip in 1942. The base was needed to refuel airplanes on their way to battle sites in Europe.

After the war, many North Americans feared a conflict with the Soviet Union. To discourage a Soviet bombing attack, a series of radar warning stations was built from Alaska to Baffin Island. Called the Distant Early Warning (DEW) Line, the stations brought

In the 1950s, some residents found jobs building stations for the Distant Early Warning (DEW) Line.

new jobs and modern technology to the people of the Northwest Territories. New communities such as Hall Beach sprang up near the radar stations.

The Canadian government urged many Aboriginal people in the Northwest Territories to leave their camps and move to settled communities.

Some Inuit moved to these communities to take jobs. But life for other Inuit was difficult. In the 1950s, disease killed entire teams of sled dogs. Without these work animals, many Inuit were unable to hunt, so they starved. Other Inuit died from tuberculosis, an illness that spread across much of the Northwest Territories at this time.

In response, the Canadian government began to build homes, schools, and hospitals for the Inuit. Gradually, Inuit hunting communities moved into permanent settlements, where most Inuit and Dene now live.

For many years, the Inuit have wanted more control over their affairs and have worked to create their own territory. In 1982 a special vote was held, and a majority of voters in the Northwest Territories chose to divide the territory in two. More than 90 percent of Inuit voters approved the idea.

Several years passed before people agreed on the exact boundary between the two territories. In 1992 a second vote was held, and the borders were approved. The new eastern territory is called Nunavut, which means "our land" in Inuktitut. The western territory has not yet been named. Leaders hope that the governments of the two new territories will be operating by 1999. One thing is certain for the people of the Northwest Territories—the seeds of change are blowing in the northern wind.

Young residents wave flags to celebrate the creation of Nunavut. This new territory will be home to about one-third of the people in the present Northwest Territories.

In remote areas with few roads, helicopters fly in supplies (above). *A gardener in the Mackenzie Valley region grows her own food* (facing page). *An artist in Gjoa Haven* (facing page inset) *makes a living by carving small sculptures.*

Communities Working Together

Up until the 1950s and 1960s, most families in the Northwest Territories relied on hunting, trapping, and fishing to make a living. Nowadays people still hunt and fish, but many also have permanent jobs that pay regular wages. Some residents do a little bit of everything to earn money. They may have a seasonal summer job guiding tourists, for example, and earn extra money selling handcrafted sculptures. Some people receive financial help from the Canadian government.

41

Mining has provided jobs in the Northwest Territories since 1938, when the first gold brick was poured in Yellowknife. Nowadays 5 percent of the workforce have jobs mining zinc, gold, lead, and silver. Most of the minerals are sold to other countries and earn a lot of money.

Thousands of barrels of oil are produced every day in Norman Wells. A long pipeline transports the fuel south to Zama, Alberta, where the mineral is refined, or purified. Oil also is pumped at Bent Horn in the Arctic Islands and at Pointed Mountain near Fort Liard.

In 1991 miners discovered diamonds near Lac de Gras on the mainland. With more finds likely, diamond mining offers a bright future for the industry.

A refinery at Norman Wells processes some of the territory's oil into fuel and other petroleum products.

The Dene and the Inuit have worried that mining might harm the environment. In the early 1970s, a mining company planned to build a pipeline through the Mackenzie Valley to carry natural gas south from the Beaufort Sea. When Canadian officials studied the plan, they found that the pipeline could change the travel patterns of game animals. Since many Dene and Inuit rely on these animals for food, the pipeline has never been built.

The fur trade is the oldest industry in the Northwest Territories. Nowadays fewer than 1 percent of workers in the territory trap fur-bearing animals for a living. These trappers provide about 10 percent of Canada's fur. Some of the animals that are caught include beavers, lynx, foxes, marten, muskrat, wolves, wolverines, and seals.

A trapper who works along the Liard River displays his furs.

Trappers in the territory once harvested 20,000 skins a year and sold the furs all over the world. But many people now are concerned about animal rights and no longer buy as many fur products. So trappers in the Northwest Territories earn less money these days.

But many people in the territory still hunt to feed their families. Moose, caribou, musk oxen, seals, whales, grouse, ducks, and geese are hunted for their meat. Artists carve figures from horns and antlers. The wool of musk oxen is spun into yarn for knitting. Selling these crafts brings in extra money for families.

A woman hangs fish to dry on wooden racks. Many people in the Northwest Territories fish and hunt for their food.

Ranchers in Hay River raise beef cattle.

Only about 4 percent of the Northwest Territories is forested, and very little of this land is used by logging companies. As a result, about 1 percent of the workforce have jobs in forestry and logging.

Because the Northwest Territories is so cold, not many crops can grow. Only about 1 percent of workers make their living from agriculture. Some growers raise vegetables in greenhouses, where the plants can survive year-round. A poultry farm near the community of Hay River produces chickens and eggs. Ranchers near Fort Smith and Hay River raise buffalo and beef cattle.

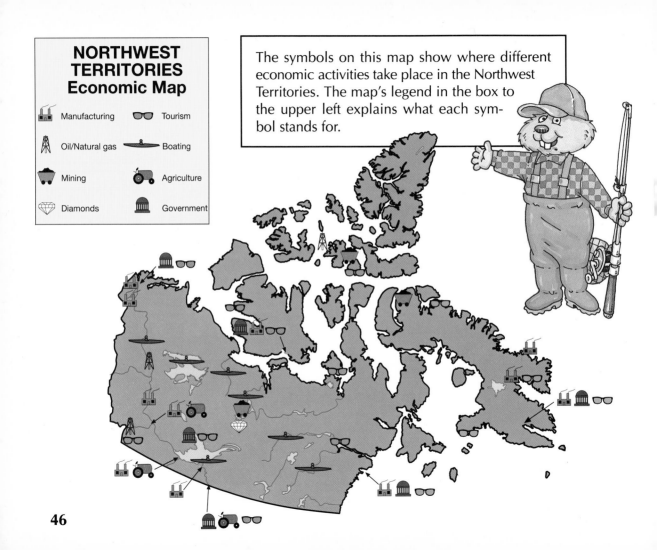

NORTHWEST TERRITORIES Economic Map

Manufacturing
Oil/Natural gas
Mining
Diamonds
Tourism
Boating
Agriculture
Government

The symbols on this map show where different economic activities take place in the Northwest Territories. The map's legend in the box to the upper left explains what each symbol stands for.

46

Workers stack lumber at a sawmill in Fort Resolution.

Manufacturing is a small part of the Northwest Territories' economy. The territory has a few sawmills, where timber is cut into boards. A small number of workers package whitefish, arctic char, and lake trout from Great Slave Lake. Fish also are packaged in the Nunavut communities of Cambridge Bay, Rankin Inlet, and Pangnirtung. Altogether about 1 percent of workers in the territory have manufacturing jobs.

With Canada's fastest growing population, the Northwest Territories has a steady need for new houses and other buildings. The construction industry provides jobs for 7 percent of the territory's workers, or about 2,000 carpenters, plumbers, electricians, bricklayers, painters, and other skilled laborers.

Long distances between communities make pilots important service workers in the Northwest Territories.

Counting government employees, about 84 percent of workers in the territory have service jobs, helping people and businesses. Shopkeepers, bankers, pilots, and airport personnel are part of the service industry. Airports are especially important in the Northwest Territories because many small communities can only be reached by airplane.

Another important service is the health care provided by doctors, nurses, and dentists. Most small communities in the Northwest Territories do not have a doctor. Instead, nurses deliver babies, prescribe medicine, and handle emergencies. People with serious injuries or illnesses usually go to hospitals in larger towns.

Every community in the territory has government service employees. Some of these workers repair roads or clear snow—a major task in the Northwest Territories! Other government workers deliver water, collect garbage, fight fires, judge cases in court, or serve as librarians or politicians.

Tourism is the fastest growing industry in the Northwest Territories. About 90,000 people visit the territory each year. Some people come to see the aurora borealis, or northern lights. These flashes of light brighten the sky in a colorful display of green, blue, red, or white. Other visitors hunt, fish, hike, canoe, camp, ski, view wildlife, or enjoy white-water rafting.

Some service workers have jobs guiding hunters and fishers. Other service workers prepare or serve food in restaurants, run lodges, or act as outfitters, supplying the equipment needed for outdoor adventure.

Many vacationers purchase arts and crafts made by Aboriginal peoples in the Northwest Territories. At co-operatives, tourists buy a variety of goods—soapstone carvings, fur dolls, jewelry, beaded moccasins, parkas, birchbark baskets, and embroidered clothing—to take a little piece of the Northwest Territories home.

An outfitter guides sport hunters through the wilderness of the Mackenzie Mountains.

Pulling on a rope, a contestant (left) *muscles his way along a snow-packed trail during a spring festival. Canoeists* (below) *race down the Mackenzie River. On a warm summer's day, three girls* (facing page) *soak up the sun at a beach in Coppermine on the Arctic coast.*

A Land of Many Cultures

The 58,000 people living in the Northwest Territories represent a variety of cultures and speak several different languages. Among the Aboriginal peoples are the Inuit, the Dene, and the Métis. These and other groups in the territory share a feeling of belonging to a unique part of the world.

A kayaker stops to rest at Bathurst Inlet.

With Aboriginal peoples making up 61 percent of the population, many residents blend traditional ways with the demands of a modern world. They may spend time during the year on the land (away from settlements) hunting animals and then come home to enjoy a video or television program.

The largest Aboriginal group in the Northwest Territories is the Inuit. The word *Inuit* means "the people" in their language of Inuktitut. Making up 37 percent of the population, the Inuit include those of the eastern Arctic as well as the Inuvialuit, who live in the northwestern part of the territory.

Most Inuit have modern homes in settled communities. Many Inuit adults hold regular jobs, while their children attend school. Televisions and radios have a place in most Inuit homes and link the North to the rest of the world.

Keeping Traditions Strong

Many Aboriginals have adjusted to the modern world while keeping their traditions strong. Although Jane Dragon, a school community counselor, and her husband lived in Fort Smith, they felt that their six children should know their cultural roots. Now that her children are grown, Mrs. Dragon looks back on the importance of the family cabin in the wilderness.

"About three times a year, we would go to our cabin. Life there was very different. We were busy all the time. The children would rise early and have breakfast. Then they would check nets with their father. With luck, they would return with whitefish, jackfish, and pickerel. The children would help gut and scale the fish. We'd have fish and bannock (a flat bread or biscuit) for lunch. Some of the fish would be smoked in our smokehouse. The scales would be used to make pictures.

"Some days the children would go hunting with their dad in the afternoon. We never took any more animals than we needed. If they found some ducks, there would be more work to do. The birds had to be cleaned, the feathers plucked, and the ducks singed to make them cleaner. After the work was done, they might go for a boat ride or, in the summer, a swim.

"In the fall, we'd go berry picking. We'd get all the berries we needed for making jam for the year. We'd always get a moose and bear. I'd use the bear grease for cooking for the rest of the year.

"In the evenings, we'd often sit by a campfire and tell the children stories about how things were in their grandparents' day. Then the eight of us would settle down in four bunk beds and go to sleep.

"It was very important to look after the environment. When we'd go back to town, we'd clean up thoroughly. If you went to our cabin today, you'd never guess that six children spent so much time there. But they did. The life on the land was good for us, so we had to teach it to our children."

Inuit light **kudliks** *(traditional soapstone lamps) to symbolize the passing of knowledge from elders to young people or from one culture to another.*

Still, the old ways are not forgotten. Teachers invite elders into classrooms to share knowledge with young students. In the summer, many Inuit live on the land in tents while they hunt caribou and musk oxen and catch trout and arctic char. Hunting and fishing provide food and materials for Inuit clothing and artwork.

Like the Inuit, most Dene live in modern communities—mainly in the western part of the territory. The Dene make up about 17 percent of the population and hold a wide variety of jobs.

A respect for the land lies at the heart of Dene culture. Like their ancestors, many Dene are hunters, trappers, and fishers. But rifles have replaced spears and bows and arrows. And fishers now use motorized boats and buy their nets instead of making them.

Most Métis in the Northwest Territories live near the Mackenzie River, the Slave River, or Great Slave Lake. The unique ancestry of the Métis combines a French, British, or Scottish background with an Aboriginal heritage. Making up 7 percent of the population, Métis people include successful artists, athletes, business owners, and politicians.

Together the Dene (above) **and Métis** (right) **make up almost one-fourth of the Northwest Territories' population.**

Non-Aboriginals of mainly European backgrounds make up about 39 percent of the population of the Northwest Territories. Many non-Aboriginals work as nurses, lawyers, teachers, or police officers. Non-Aboriginals traditionally have held most of the skilled jobs because many Aboriginals lacked the necessary training. But this is changing rapidly as Aboriginal peoples receive more formal education.

The future Nunavut is home to about one-third of the people in the present Northwest Territories. Around 80 percent of the residents of Nunavut are Inuit. In the future western territory,

Square dancers perform on Nunavut Day, which celebrates the founding of the North's new territory.

the population is more varied. About half of the residents are non-Aboriginal. Dene, Métis, and Inuvialuit make up the rest of the region's population.

The varied heritage of the Northwest Territories' people comes to life in more than 20 museums and cultural centers. The best known of these is the Prince of Wales Northern Heritage Centre in Yellowknife. The museum's displays feature the history, exploration, cultures, and transportation of the North. Many Dene and Inuit artworks also are exhibited.

Festivals take place across the Northwest Territories. In Iqaluit, people at the Toonik Tyme festival celebrate the arrival of spring with traditional Inuit singing and dancing, snowhouse building, ice sculpting, and animal skinning contests.

Mushers show their skill at the popular Caribou Carnival in Yellowknife.

The Sahtu Dene Games in Deline (Fort Franklin) feature drum dancing, games and contests, making bannock (a type of bread), and tea brewing. The Caribou Carnival in Yellowknife includes ice sculpting and a dogsled race. Runners from all over North America head to Nanisivik to participate in the Midnight Sun Marathon—the world's northernmost marathon.

Each summer the Great Northern Arts Festival takes place in Inuvik. Artists and musicians from throughout the Northwest Territories gather to share their work and watch live performances and artists' demonstrations.

Every two years, the territory sends more than 300 athletes to the Arctic Winter Games to compete against participants from Alaska, Russia, Greenland, the Yukon, and northern Alberta. The contests, which sometimes are held in the Northwest Territories, include indoor soccer, figure skating, cross-country skiing, dogsled racing, and snowshoe racing. One popular activity is the high kick, in which competitors leap into the air to kick a piece of seal-skin suspended by a string.

All of these special events allow the people of the Northwest Territories to come together in a spirit of teamwork and goodwill. At the same time, residents share their unique cultural heritages with one another and with people from other northern lands.

White-water rafting (facing page left), *golfing* (facing page right), *and hiking* (right) *are just a few of the fun outdoor activities enjoyed by residents and tourists alike in the Northwest Territories.*

Famous People of the Northwest Territories

1 **Susan Aglukark** (born 1967) is a singer and songwriter from Arviat. She records her songs, which deal with modern Inuit life, in English and in Inuktitut. Aglukark, whose albums include the well-known *Arctic Rose,* was named top new star at the 1994 Canadian Country Music Awards.

2 **John Amagoalik** (born 1947), former president of an Inuit political and cultural organization called the Inuit Tapirisat of Canada, grew up in Resolute. In 1993 he was chosen to lead the Nunavut Implementation Commission, which is helping to design the new territory's government.

3 **Kenojuak Ashevak** (born 1927), an artist from Cape Dorset, is best known for her drawings of birds. In 1967 she received the Order of Canada, a national award for achievement. Her most famous print, *The Enchanted Owl,* was reproduced on a Canadian postage stamp in 1970.

4 **Pitseolak Ashoona** (1904–1983) was known for her drawings of traditional Inuit life. Born on Nottingham Island, she told her story in the book *Pitseolak: Pictures out of My Life.* She received the Order of Canada in 1977.

George Blondin (born 1922) is an author known for *When the World Was New,* a book of Dene legends. Born at Horton Lake, Northwest Territories, he has worked as a newspaper columnist, a miner, and a hunter and trapper. Blondin also has served as vice president of the Dene Nation and as chair of the Denendeh Elders' Council.

6 **Ethel Blondin-Andrew** (born 1951) has been a teacher, language specialist, and territorial deputy minister. In 1988 she became the first Aboriginal woman elected to Canada's House of Commons. She was appointed to the cabinet as the secretary of state in 1993. Blondin-Andrew was born in Fort Norman, Northwest Territories.

7 **Nellie Cournoyea** (born 1940) was a member of the legislative assembly of the Northwest Territories for 13 years. In 1992 the assembly elected her premier of the territory—the first Aboriginal and the first woman to hold such a position in Canada. Cournoyea was born in Aklavik.

■ **Andrew Dexter** (born 1975) holds two world records in power lifting. In 1994 he hoisted 574 pounds (260 kilograms), or three times his own body weight. Dexter is a resident of Fort Smith.

9 **Clennell Haggerston ("Punch") Dickins** (born 1899), was a pioneer bush pilot who flew long distances across the Northwest Territories. In 1929 he became the first pilot to land north of the Arctic Circle when he brought mail by plane to the community of Aklavik. Dickins received important awards, including the Order of Canada in 1968.

9

10

10 **Georges Erasmus** (born 1948) was president of the Dene Nation from 1976 to 1985, after which he served as national chief of the Assembly of First Nations until 1991. Born in Fort Rae, Northwest Territories, he was appointed a member of the Order of Canada in 1987 for his dedication to the rights of Aboriginal peoples in Canada and throughout the world.

11 **Etuangat** (born 1900; left in photo) is a respected elder, carver, whaler, and storyteller in Pangnirtung. He saved many lives by bringing sick or injured people who lived on the land (away from settled communities) to the hospital in Pangnirtung by dogsled.

■ **Sharon and Shirley Firth** (born 1953), twin sisters born on the land in the Mackenzie Valley, were members of the Canadian National Cross-Country Ski Team in the 1970s and 1980s. Award-winning athletes, the Firths skied in four Olympic Games and were honored with the Order of Canada in 1984.

■ **Jim Green** (born 1943), originally from Alberta, is a longtime resident of the Northwest Territories. He has worked as a radio broadcaster, journalist, and storyteller. Green, who lives in Fort Smith, has published two books of poetry—*North Book* and *Beyond Here*—and is writing a book about Fort Smith's history.

14 **Rosemary Kuptana** (born 1953) was the first female president of the Inuit Broadcasting Corporation, which produces Inuit television shows. From Sachs Harbour, Northwest Territories, she was awarded the Order of Canada in 1988.

15 **Michael Kusugak** (born 1948), a children's book writer, lives in Rankin Inlet. His most famous book, *A Promise Is a Promise,* was co-written with celebrated children's author Robert Munsch. Kusugak's other titles include *Northern Lights: The Soccer Trails* and *Baseball Bats for Christmas.*

■ **Cece McCauley** grew up near the shores of Great Bear Lake and has worked as a businesswoman, columnist, politician, and artist. When elected chief of the Inuvik Dene Band in 1978, she became the first female band chief in the Northwest Territories.

17 **Helen Mamayaok Maksagak** (born 1931) served as deputy commissioner of the Northwest Territories from 1992 until 1995, when she was appointed commissioner of the territory. Born near Coppermine, she is the first Inuit and the first woman to hold this position.

■ **Markoosie** (born 1941) originally from northern Québec, moved to Resolute at a young age. The first Inuit bush pilot, he also became the first Inuit to publish a novel. The story, *Harpoon of the Hunter,* describes a hunt for a rabid polar bear.

19 **Guy Mary-Rousselière** (1913–1994), known to the Inuit as "Ataata Mari" (or "Father Mary"), spent more than 50 years as a Catholic missionary in Pond Inlet. An archaeologist, he wrote books and articles about his work in the Northwest Territories.

20 **Jessie Oonark** (1906–1985), a widely recognized artist, is known for her prints and tapestries. Some of her work is on display at the National Arts Centre in Ottawa, Ontario. Named in her honor, the Jessie Oonark Centre stands in the town of Baker Lake, Northwest Territories, where Oonark lived for many years.

21 **Jack Sissons** (1892–1969) served from 1955 until 1966 as the first judge of the Territorial Court of the Northwest Territories. Insisting that people be tried by and in their own communities, he flew his court 20,000 miles (32,000 km) each year to bring justice "to every man's door." Sissons encouraged Inuit artists to make carvings of his most famous cases, and these artworks are now on display in Yellowknife. For his efforts to help Inuit people, Sissons was given the Inuit name Ekoktoegee ("The One Who Listens").

Fast Facts

Territorial Symbols

Flower: mountain avens
Tree: jack pine
Bird: gyrfalcon
Tartan: white for the snow, green for the forests, yellow for the birch trees in the fall, and blue for the many lakes, rivers, and oceans.

Territorial Highlights

Landmarks: Auyuittuq National Park on Baffin Island, Ellesmere Island National Park, Nahanni National Park on the western mainland, Aulavik National Park on Banks Island, Waterfalls Route along the Mackenzie Highway, Thelon Game Sanctuary near Baker Lake, Kekerten Historic Park near Pangnirtung, Bathurst Inlet Lodge, Northwest Passage Historic Park in Gjoa Haven, Native Theatre Group in Yellowknife, Tunooniq Theatre in Pond Inlet, West Baffin Eskimo Co-operative in Cape Dorset, Baker Lake Inuit Camp near Baker Lake, Prince of Wales Northern Heritage Centre in Yellowknife

Annual events: Sunrise Festival in Inuvik (Jan.), Cabin Fever Days in Fort Liard (March), Caribou Carnival in Yellowknife (March), Canadian Championship Dog Derby on Great Slave Lake (March), Toonik Tyme in Iqaluit (April), Beluga Jamboree in Tuktoyaktuk (April), Umingmak Frolics in Cambridge Bay (May), Midway Lake Music Festival near Fort McPherson (June), Great Northern Arts Festival in Inuvik (July), Sahtu Dene Games in Deline (August)

Population

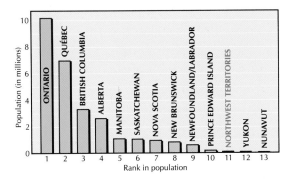

Population*: 58,000
Rank in population, nationwide: 11th
Population distribution: 37 percent urban; 63 percent rural
Population density: 46.3 people per 1,000 sq mi (17.9 per 1,000 sq km)
Capital: Yellowknife (15,179)
Major communities (and populations*): Iqaluit (3,552), Hay River (3,206), Inuvik (3,206), Fort Smith (2,480), Rankin Inlet (1,706), Rae-Edzo (1,521), Arviat (1,323), Baker Lake (1,186), Fort Simpson (1,142)
Major ethnic groups*: non-Aboriginals, 39 percent; Inuit, 37 percent; Dene, 17 percent; Métis, 7 percent
*1991 census

Endangered and Threatened Species

Mammals: Peary caribou, beluga whale, wood bison
Birds: whooping crane, Eskimo curlew, anatum peregrine falcon
Fish: shortjaw cisco, Great Lakes deepwater sculpin

Geographic Highlights

Area (land/water): 1,322,902 sq mi (3,426,320 sq km)
Rank in area, nationwide: 1st (including Nunavut)
Highest point: Mount Sir James MacBrien (9,062 ft/ 2,762 m)
Major lakes: Great Bear, Great Slave, Nettilling
Major rivers: Mackenzie, Coppermine, Slave, Hay, Burnside, Back, Thelon, Kazan

Economy

Percentage of Workers Per Job Sector

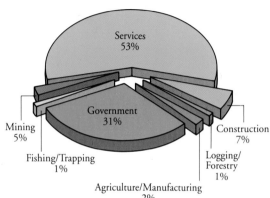

Services 53%
Government 31%
Mining 5%
Fishing/Trapping 1%
Construction 7%
Logging/Forestry 1%
Agriculture/Manufacturing 2%

Natural resources: wildlife, oil, natural gas, gold, zinc, lead, nickel, copper, silver, tungsten, diamonds
Agricultural products: vegetables, chickens, eggs, buffalo, and beef cattle
Manufactured goods: petroleum products, food products, wood products, printed materials, soapstone sculptures, embroidered clothing, paintings, prints

Energy

Electric power: diesel fuel oil (50 percent), hydroelectric (50 percent)

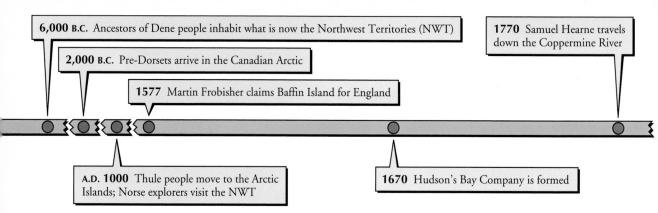

6,000 B.C. Ancestors of Dene people inhabit what is now the Northwest Territories (NWT)

2,000 B.C. Pre-Dorsets arrive in the Canadian Arctic

1577 Martin Frobisher claims Baffin Island for England

1770 Samuel Hearne travels down the Coppermine River

A.D. 1000 Thule people move to the Arctic Islands; Norse explorers visit the NWT

1670 Hudson's Bay Company is formed

Federal Government

Capital: Ottawa

Head of state: British Crown, represented by the governor general

Head of government: prime minister

Cabinet: ministers appointed by the prime minister

Parliament: Senate—104 members appointed by the governor general; House of Commons—295 members elected by the people

Northwest Territories representation in parliament: 1 senator; 2 house members

Voting age: 18

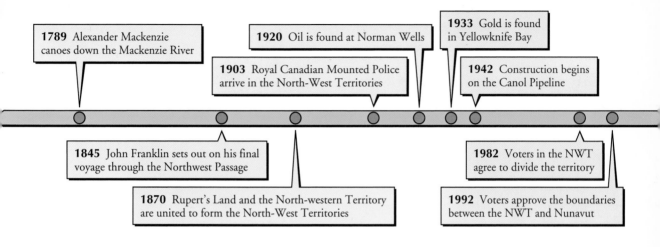

1789 Alexander Mackenzie canoes down the Mackenzie River

1920 Oil is found at Norman Wells

1933 Gold is found in Yellowknife Bay

1903 Royal Canadian Mounted Police arrive in the North-West Territories

1942 Construction begins on the Canol Pipeline

1845 John Franklin sets out on his final voyage through the Northwest Passage

1982 Voters in the NWT agree to divide the territory

1870 Rupert's Land and the North-western Territory are united to form the North-West Territories

1992 Voters approve the boundaries between the NWT and Nunavut

Territorial Government

Capital: Yellowknife
Chief executive officer: commissioner
Head of government: premier
Cabinet: 8 members chosen by and from the Legislative Assembly
Legislative Assembly: 24 elected members
Voting age: 18

Government Services

To help pay the people who work for the Northwest Territories' government, the people of the Northwest Territories pay taxes on money they earn and on many of the items they buy. The services run by the territorial government help assure residents of a high quality of life. Government funds pay for medical care, for education, for road building and repairs, and for other facilities such as libraries and parks. In addition, the government has funds to help people who are disabled, elderly, or poor.

Glossary

desert An area of land that receives only about 10 inches (25 cm) or less of rain or snow a year.

fjord A deep, narrow inlet of the sea lying between steep cliffs.

glacier A large body of ice and snow that flows down mountain valleys, often following paths originally formed by rivers. The term is also used to refer to masses of ice that move slowly over land.

ice age A period when ice caps cover large regions of the earth. The term *Ice Age* usually refers to the most recent one, called the Pleistocene, which began almost 2 million years ago and ended about 10,000 years ago.

ice cap A very thick, slow-moving glacier that covers large areas of a continent.

missionary A person sent out by a religious group to spread its beliefs to other people.

permafrost Ground that remains permanently frozen. A shallow layer of surface soil may thaw during the summer, but the ground below does not.

precipitation Rain, snow, and other forms of moisture that fall to earth.

reserve Public land set aside by the government to be used by Aboriginal peoples.

treaty An agreement between two or more groups, usually having to do with peace or trade.

tundra A treeless plain found in Arctic and subarctic regions. The ground beneath the top layer of soil is permanently frozen, but the topsoil thaws for a short period each summer, allowing mosses, lichens, and dwarf shrubs to grow.

Pronunciation Guide

Arviat (AHR-vee-aht)

Chipewyan (chih-puh-WY-uhn)

Dene (day-NAY)

Inuit (EE-noo-eet)

Inuktitut (ee-NOOK-tih-toot)

Inuvik (ih-NOO-vihk)

Métis (may-TEE)

Nanisivik (nan-uh-SIH-vihk)

Pangnirtung (pang-NYU-tung)

Thelon (THEE-lahn)

Thule (TOO-lee)

Index

About the Author

Richard Daitch has lived in Canada since the early 1970s. Before turning to writing, he worked as an elementary, junior high, and high school teacher as well as an assistant principal and principal in various communities of Canada's arctic and subarctic regions. His books include *Flee on Your Donkey, The Boy Who Returned,* and a series of educational publications entitled *Jim Kilabuk Remembers.* Daitch lives with his wife and two daughters in Fort Smith, Northwest Territories.

Acknowledgments

Mapping Specialists Ltd., pp. 1, 12, 13, 36; Ned Therrien, pp. 2, 8, 10, 14, 17 (left and right), 49; Artwork by Terry Boles, pp. 6, 12, 46, 65; © Lyn Hancock, pp. 7, 11, 15, 16, 20, 21 (left and right), 22 (left), 39, 40, 41 (both), 42, 43, 44, 45, 47, 48, 50 (left and right), 51, 52, 54, 55 (left and right), 57, 58 (left and right), 59, 60 (top left), 62 (center), 68, 69; David Dvorak, Jr. p. 9 (left); Travel Arctic, pp. 9 (right), 19 (bottom—Dan Heringa), 38; John Edward Hayashida, p. 19 (top); National Archives of Canada, p. 22 (left—C16328), 26 (C1045), 34 (PA102598), 36 (right—PA101813), 61 (center—C57671), 63 (center—PA179281); Mirror Syndication International, p. 25; The Bodleian Library, University of Oxford (Poole Portrait 50), p. 27; Hudson's Bay Company Archives, Provincial Archives of Manitoba, p. 29; Library of Congress, p. 30, 32; Confederation Life Gallery of Canadian History, p. 31; Artwork by Laura Westlund, p. 32; J.H.A. Wilmot/Hudson's Bay Company Archives, Provincial Archives of Manitoba, p. 33; Artwork by John Erste, pp. 35, 53; Henry Busse/NWT Archives, p. 36 (left); Eric Watt/NWT Archives, p. 37; Leena Evic-Twerdin/Nunavut Tunngavik Inc., p. 56; Terry Pearce/Nunavut Implementation Commission, p. 60 (top right); Inuit Art Section, p. 60 (center and bottom—bottom by Jimmy Manning), 62 (top—by Hunter George), 63 (bottom left); The Honourable Ethel Blondin-Andrew's Office, p. 61 (top left); Government of the Northwest Territories, p. 61 (top right); Royal Commission on Aboriginal Peoples, p. 61 (bottom); William Belsey, p. 62 (bottom); Tessa MacIntosh/Office of the Commissioner of the Northwest Territories, p. 63 (top); Busse/NWT Archives, p. 63 (right); Travel Arctic, GNWT, p. 71.